PLANTING WILDFLOWERS

A Grower's Guide to
Welcoming the Wild

Foxglove, Tree Bumblebee & snail

PLANTING WILDFLOWERS

A Grower's Guide to
Welcoming the Wild

JANE MOORE

COVER AND CHAPTER OPENER ILLUSTRATIONS
BY JAMES WESTON LEWIS

INTERNAL ILLUSTRATIONS
BY CLAIRE HARRUP

Hardie Grant

QUADRILLE

CONTENTS

Herb Robert & hoverfly

For my Cannington College lecturers
and classmates

Wildflowers are little wonders of nature; they are born survivors, exploiting the most unfavourable pavement cracks to grow, colonising wasteland, and pioneering in the inhospitable aftermath of war, drought, and even nuclear contamination. These tiny spirits are often important signs of hope, and many are instantly recognisable, even if their names may spring less readily to mind. Their delicate strength and adaptability make them good plants for the garden – easy to grow, tough and dependable. They also appear in numerous folk tales, are fantastic for wildlife, and their beauty and simplicity have the uncanny ability to remind you of childhood.

Wildflowers are everywhere you look. Whatever your level of experience, you can take an interest in them. Even if you don't have a garden, or live in an urban environment, in a flat or apartment, there are sure to be wildflowers nearby.

Wildflowers are wonderful to see, whether in drifts of English hay meadows or stretching for miles across the great prairies of the USA, but they're equally beautiful in isolation. The delicate tissue paper petals of a wild poppy or the winter silhouette of a teasel are every bit as lovely as the masses of wild flora carpeting the wide-open spaces of national parks, woodlands and wildernesses.

Many of these little beauties grow anywhere with little effort, although it's vital to be careful of some, as they can be invasive. I love seeing the giant Rosebay Willowherb – one of the first plants I ever learned to recognise as it colonised a building plot near my childhood home – but I wouldn't want it in my tiny urban garden, as it would rapidly dominate everything else. There is such a thing as the right plant for the right place, even with wildflowers, so my tastes run to the daintier Snake's Head Fritillary, poppies and cornflowers – or Bachelor's Buttons, if you're in the USA. That's another lovely thing about wildflowers – their common names are wonderfully evocative, often varying from country to country, and even locality to locality. Queen Anne's Lace in the UK is not the same as Queen Anne's Lace in the USA, but both plants are wildflowers, although the USA version is regarded as a nuisance in some states. Which just goes to show that one person's wildflower is another person's weed. It's a question of interpretation.

All flowers, except those that are bred and cultivated, such as F1 hybrids, are wildflowers somewhere in the world. Whether you should plant non-native wildflowers is up to you. Purists argue you should only grow local species of native wildflowers, but try telling that to a bumblebee enjoying a late-flowering cosmos in your garden. As always, it's best to make informed decisions that you yourself are happy with. To that end, I have tried to give the best information I can in this book. It's not comprehensive – I couldn't possibly include every wildflower I wanted and there are many wildflowers specific to woodlands, seashores, highlands, moors and mountains that I haven't touched upon. Instead, I have included the easy to grow, essential to know, instantly recognisable and, in some cases infamous, wildflowers that I love. That leaves you with plenty more to discover as your wildflower fascination grows.

CHAPTER ONE

WHY GROW YOUR OWN WILDFLOWERS?

There are so many reasons why growing wildflowers is a good idea. For one, it's great for the planet, especially for the animals and insects that rely on them. Many different habitats are threatened throughout the world, along with the naturally occurring flora they support and the insects and animals that are often utterly dependent on them. Just think of the amazing Monarch butterfly and its epic trek from Canada to Mexico, which spans several generations, all of them dependent on humble milkweed for their caterpillar food plant. As farming has become more intense, milkweed has been weeded out, threatening the Monarch's survival. Now, however, a popular movement across the USA is encouraging people to plant milkweed in their gardens specifically to support the Monarch butterfly.

This is just one example of how important planting wildflowers can be. milkweed isn't much to look at unless you're a monarch butterfly, and many wildflowers might not be your first choice for planting a beautiful garden. But you'll be surprised just how many are truly lovely, making your space look great, as well as benefitting the insects, animals and wild creatures that rely on them.

SO, WHY GROW WILDFLOWERS IN YOUR GARDEN?

First, because it's easy. Wildflowers have evolved to make the most of certain conditions and if your garden possesses those conditions, they will thrive. That makes wildflowers a great choice for difficult gardens. If your garden is exposed and windy, or has thin, dry soil, you'll have no trouble finding numerous wildflowers that just love to grow there. The same goes if your garden is shady, dark and damp.

Second, you should grow wildflowers because they are tough. These dainty little lovelies are made of stern stuff, coping with all sorts of weather: wind, rain, floods and even fire. In the wild, they sometimes seem to fade away for a few years, only to pop up again when the right climactic conditions coincide, flourishing against the odds.

Last, grow wildflowers because they form part of a vibrant ecosystem and make themselves invaluable to the garden. They'll not only bring in bees and insects, but also birds and tiny mammals that feed on their seeds, plus the birds and predators that feed on the insects. Many plants and insects evolve together in a mutually beneficial way, so by planting local wildflower species, you're helping the local wildlife in more ways than you might expect. Just remember that beautiful Monarch butterfly and plain old milkweed.

WHAT EXACTLY IS A 'WILDFLOWER'?

A true wildflower is a plant that grows in the wild – it wasn't deliberately grown or intentionally seeded or planted and it is native to the place where it grows. That usually means no cultivars, hybrids or varieties and no double or fancy flowers. But 'wildflower' is a bit of a catch-all term for many species that, despite being classed as wildflowers in one part of the globe, aren't necessarily local to that particular location. That's not to say you shouldn't plant those lovely ready-made wildflower mixes that often contain non-native species – bees and birds aren't fussy where their nectar and seeds come from. 'Native' is a better term for many true wildflowers, which is to say plants that are specific to a country, such as English bluebells. But you can hone in even more narrowly and more locally with species that occur in very small, very specific areas, such as the 'Cheddar Pink' in Somerset, local to the famous gorge. UK charity Plantlife has sought to spread awareness of these local treasures with its County Flowers scheme, highlighting local and sometimes endangered species as county emblems.

Other equally valid ways of describing wildflowers include 'naturalised' species – those considered natives because they have been in an area for so long. Take the snowdrop in the UK, for example (see page 123), or the common weed ground elder, which was brought to Britain by the Romans as a vegetable and is now the bane of many gardeners' lives. You might also come across 'introduced' species – either those that were introduced deliberately and then escaped into the wild, such as Oxeye Daisy in the USA, or those that simply arrived accidentally and then established themselves because of their sheer invasiveness. A good example of this is the Himalayan Balsam in the UK, a pretty but persistent plant with explosive seedpods that you'll spot around rivers and watercourses. These 'invasive' plants can cause significant issues in their non-native habitats, out-competing local flora and creating long-term problems.

The water hyacinth is a text-book example of this. Originally from the Amazon Basin in South America, it's now considered an invasive plant in more than 50 countries, blocking waterways and even entire lakes, depleting their oxygen and providing breeding grounds for mosquitoes. Shockingly, this attractive little plant was still widely available to buy until recently, despite the fact that it is virtually uncontainable. The global infestation was originally thought to have been brought about by people disposing of unwanted pond and aquarium plants, and by recreational boats.

This all goes to show how vitally important it is to preserve native wildflowers. The good news is that this isn't difficult, as wildflowers are so easy to grow. Choose the plants that grow naturally in the fields and woods around your home and they will happily grow in your garden too. They might not be as showy as a garden flower, but there are few plants prettier that Meadow Cranesbill (*Geranium pratense*) with its delicate, summer-sky blue flowers rising above its finely cut leaves. Besides, many garden plants are often selected variations of native wildflowers. One of my favourite geraniums for the garden is *Geranium pratense* 'Mrs Kendall Clark', which is almost exactly the same as the wild form but with ice-blue flowers. You'd be surprised just how many of our 'garden' flowers are just variations on the flowers that grow wild around us.

WHERE DO WILDFLOWERS GROW NATURALLY?

Wildflowers grow everywhere. Look around and you'll spot flowers popping up in cracks in pavements, on odd bits of waste ground, building sites, and even on rooftops and in guttering. These are the opportunists – grabbing a small foothold from which to flower and reproduce. Although not perhaps as spectacular as the huge swathes of flowers you see sweeping across the wild hills and mountains in pictures, they're every bit as important, simply because they're found in towns and cities, providing pollen, nectar and seeds for the wildlife that eke out an existence in this inhospitable environment. And this is precisely why our gardens play such a huge role in the urban ecosystem.

Wildflowers are specially adapted to their individual environments – often uniquely so. If you want to be absolutely purist about seeding an area of wildflowers, you should collect the seed from the field next door so its provenance is as local as can be. In fact, many organisations do exactly this – the National Trust in the UK for example. That way you can be absolutely certain that the squinancywort of Dorset stays local rather than mingling with the squinancywort of Norfolk. While both might appear to be exactly the same plant, they aren't. To a botanist, each species has subtle but important differences that allow it to thrive and survive.

These wildflowers are often very specific to their location – a harebell in Scotland may be subtly different from one in Wales, for instance – and some of these variations may go back ages. One of my favourite examples is Irish heather. You may think of heather as a predominantly Scottish native, but Irish heather is native to Ireland and Spain, and bears visibly distinct differences from Scottish heather, although they are related – they've simply evolved differently over time.

They're also specific to their environment. You won't find that harebell, whether Scottish or Welsh, growing in a woodland setting. It thrives in sunny, breezy, coastal climates, while ferns, wood anemones and iconic English bluebells are more typical of the UK's deciduous forests.

So far, so UK-centric. Go to the European Alps, the Greek islands or to western Australia and you'll find even more flowers that are so specific to their area. In the US, many of the wildflowers that populate the prairies, hills, mountains and deserts of its hugely different states would simply not grow in other parts of the country, let alone anywhere else. Strangely, though, many of those prairie wildflowers have become hugely popular border plants in Europe. Black-Eyed Susan (*Rudbeckia*), Coneflower (*Echinacea*) and Tickseed (*Coreopsis*) are brilliant border plants that are as beneficial to European wildlife as they are to bees and butterflies in the US. Which just goes to show that, where one person sees a wildflower, another sees an annoying weed. And equally, what matters most for some is, native or not, the amount of good a wildflower offers the local wildlife.

WHY ARE WILDFLOWERS IMPORTANT?

Sit quietly and watch a meadow for just five minutes and it's plain to see that wildflowers are hugely important to the natural world. You'll soon hear the buzz of insects – wild populations of bees, butterflies, moths and other less glamorous species. Flowers provide nectar and pollen as well as shelter, somewhere to lay eggs, and, for butterflies and moths, a place to pupate. With all that activity, it's no surprise you'll also see birds flitting over the meadow, picking off the insects, with many taking the seeds from the finished flowers later in the season. Rodents, such as mice, also appreciate the seeds, while predators, like falcons and foxes, appreciate the mice. This ecological circle of life all starts with your patch of wildflowers.

That patch doesn't need to be big, but it does need to be wild. A study from the University of Leeds found that gardens with manicured lawns and lots of bedding and cultivated plants were far less attractive to bees than those with untreated lawns, so clover was abundant, and borders with weeds such as nettles and perhaps the odd bramble. The problem is that many cultivated plants bear little or no pollen, and that while double flowers may be showy, they have minimal appeal to bees. Take bedding plants, for example – many are F1 hybrids, which ensure uniformity and vigour, but offer nothing in terms of pollen, nectar or seed. Rather than those flamboyant African or French marigolds, it's far better for the bees if you grow a single-flowered pot marigold with all that lovely pollen, followed by clusters of seeds later in the season.

It may not seem like you're making a big difference, but you are. Gardens count for a significant amount of the green space in cities, and the cumulative impact of how they are managed makes an enormous difference to wildlife populations locally. The study found that gardens in Leeds counted for almost a third, 30 per cent, of the green space in the city. Across England as a whole, urban areas occupy 10 per cent of the land surface, of which between 20 and 40 per cent of that is garden. Just think about the wildlife potential of all those gardens – and it all starts with a handful of wildflowers.

WILDFLOWER FOLKLORE

DANDELION

You're probably so used to seeing dandelions
everywhere in spring that you've almost stopped
noticing them. These sunny little flowers are regarded
as persistent weeds and a bit of a nuisance by many,
and an awful lot of time and money is spent trying
to rid lawns of them – usually with only partial success.
Nonetheless, the cheery, unstoppable dandelion is
as old as the hills, with its herbal uses recorded on
ancient tablets in China and Egypt, and its origins
steeped in folklore.

Greek legend has it that dandelions were born of the
dust raised by the passage of Apollo's chariot across the
sun, which is why they open at first light and close at
dusk. In another Greek myth, Theseus ate dandelions
for 30 days to give him strength before his battle with
the Minotaur. Others have termed the dandelion
the 'Shepherd's Clock' because of the way its petals

open and shut with the sun, while we always called dandelion seed heads 'clocks' when I was a child. Those seeds, which float on the breeze, populating gardens and roadsides with even more dandelions, mean the plant has long been associated with growth and transformation, while others have it that you can rid yourself of bad habits or thoughts by blowing away the seeds on a dandelion clock.

The name 'dandelion' comes from the Norman French '*dents de lion*', or lion's teeth, a reference to its jagged, toothed leaves. The fact that this little flower has so many other names – including 'Lion's Tooth', 'Blow Ball', 'Priest Crown', 'Bitter Wort' and the wonderful 'Swine Snort' – reflects its significance in people's hearts. There's also the French colloquial name 'Pisse-en-lit', which comes from the fact that, as well as making a tasty addition to salads, young dandelion leaves are known for their diuretic qualities, meaning you might not want to eat too many!

BEES AND PLANTS

The connection between bees and plants goes almost without saying. The two are mutually dependent on one another, to the benefit of both. It's a simple exchange: flowers provide bees with nectar and pollen, essential to feeding their colony, while bees help flowers reproduce by spreading pollen from one plant to another.

Bees feed on the nectar of flowers, which is specially produced to attract bees and other insects. As they arrive, they become covered in pollen, a powder that contains the plant's male genetic material. They then spread this to other flowers they visit, so pollinating them, allowing the plant to set seed and reproduce itself. Without the bee's activity, this cycle of pollination and reproduction would be almost impossible. Although there are other pollinators, including butterflies and moths, as well as some birds and bats, it's predominantly bees that perform this vital function.

Honey bees are probably the best-known bees, although they only make up a small part of the 20,000 or so bee species. In the USA and Canada alone, there are 3,600 native species, and that doesn't include honey bees, which were brought from Europe. Bumblebees, especially, are hugely important pollinators, particularly of agricultural crops and wildflowers, but the many species of solitary bee also play a huge role. While lots of bee species are happy to take nectar and pollen

from all sorts of plants, some bees are specific to one sort of flowering plant. For example, there is a bee specific to ivy that feeds from ivy flowers, while the Bee Orchid is specially adapted to make itself attractive to its bee pollinator.

CHAPTER TWO

WHAT CAN I GROW IN MY GARDEN?

G rowing wildflowers in your own garden doesn't mean your garden needs to be messy and wild. Many wildflowers can be incorporated into beds and borders where they will flower beautifully and look lovely. You might be surprised just how many 'wildflowers' are available at garden centres and nurseries simply as lovely plants for the border.

There are lots of different ways you can grow wildflowers, and lots of different types you can grow, but by far the easiest is to simply grow a few quick and easy annuals. The super thing about annuals is that you can drop a plant or two, or a sprinkle of seeds, into a pot or container, or even into beds and borders with the odd gap. Annuals are amazingly keen to grow and tolerate less than ideal conditions, which means you should get good results without too much trouble. The selection on pages 32–37 is by no means exhaustive – it's my list of go-to plants for colour, floweriness and fortitude. But don't be afraid to try some of the other favourites I've highlighted too. Steer clear of anything too rare and difficult, though – it's not practical or possible to cultivate wild orchids from a quick sprinkle of seeds, for example.

THREE WAYS TO GROW WILDFLOWERS FROM SEED

SOW DIRECTLY INTO THE GROUND

This is by far the easiest method and simply requires clearing a bare patch of soil, removing any weeds and then tickling it up a little to create a fine crumbly surface. You can either scatter a few seeds or, for a larger space, create shallow drills no more than 1cm (½in) deep, spaced about 20cm (8in) apart. Water beforehand if the soil is dry, but definitely water the seeds afterwards as this helps them to contact with the soil, which is essential for germination. This method works brilliantly for more robust, meadow species, such as poppies, cornflowers and corncockle. It's a very effective way to grow foxgloves too.

SOW IN POTS

This is an excellent way to grow species that need a bit more nurturing or that are longer-term propositions, such as foxgloves, which take two years to flower. Growing in pots allows you to keep a close eye on watering and to decide where to plant your flowers at a later date, by which time they will also be bigger, stronger plants.

SOW IN PLUG TRAYS

Plug trays are a marvellous halfway house system for growing many wildflowers, offering some of the nurturing you get with pot sowing combined with speedy planting. Sowing in plug trays is economical on seed, but you need to plant out as soon as the plant roots start filling the plug, as they will quickly die if stressed. Alternatively, pot them on into larger pots. I love growing masses of cowslips and primroses in this way.

TEN EASY-TO-GROW ANNUAL WILDFLOWERS

CORNFLOWER OR **BACHELOR'S BUTTONS**
Centaurea cyanus

The wild cornflower has brilliant blue flowers in summer although these also occasionally appear pink or white. As well as looking great in the border, they are fantastic for cutting.

GROWING TIPS: Sow directly into well-drained soil in a sunny spot from March to May for flowers from June to September.

POPPY
Papaver rhoeas

A field of wild poppies is a glorious sight in early summer and also brilliant for bees. Poppies always appear when the soil is disturbed, for example after the soil is ploughed.

GROWING TIPS: Sow directly into well-drained, poor soil in a sunny spot from March to May for flowers in August and September, or sow in late summer for early flowers the following year.

CORNCOCKLE
Agrostemma githago

The stately and elegant corncockle, with its beautiful mauve flowers, used to be a common sight in European cornfields but is now critically endangered, which makes it a must-grow wildflower to my mind.

GROWING TIPS: Sow directly into well-drained, poor soil in a sunny spot in March or April for flowers in August and September. If growing in the border, you'll need to stake the 1m (3ft) tall stems and keep deadheading – but allow the last flowers to set seed as plants will self-seed given the opportunity.

FOXGLOVE
Digitalis purpurea

Who doesn't love a foxglove, with its tall spikes of spotted purple or white flowers? It is a biennial though, which means it only produces leaves the first year and flowers the next. But it self-seeds freely, so you should get a lovely succession of flowers coming through year after year. Brilliant for bees, especially bumblebees, which sometimes roost overnight in the tubular flowers.

GROWING TIPS: Sow directly in situ or into trays and pots at any time of the year, then plant out in a lightly shaded spot – they're perfect for shady borders and dappled sunshine spots. Foxgloves enjoy disturbed soil, which is why you often see them popping up on building sites and waste ground.

VIPER'S BUGLOSS
Echium vulgare

This is a biennial, and it's worth growing for its spectacular cobalt blue flowers, which start off pink in the bud. It flowers from June to September and is ideal for particularly dry, thin, parched soils, where it attracts all sorts of bees and butterflies.

GROWING TIPS: Sow directly into well-drained, poor soil in a sunny spot at any time of year.

TICKSEED
Coreopsis tinctoria

This easy-growing, long-flowering annual sometimes lasts a few years in the right spot and self-seeds freely if allowed – sometimes too freely in its native USA. The big, daisy-like flowers are great for bees and other pollinators.

GROWING TIPS: Sow seeds in pots or trays and plant in a sunny spot. Tickseed copes with most soil types, but especially likes moister soils.

FIDDLENECK
Phacelia tanacetifolia

As popular in Europe as it is in its native USA, 'Lacy Phacelia' is often spotted growing as a cover crop or green manure in market gardens. In gardens, it's incredibly attractive to bees and other insects, and its dense, curled lavender-blue flowers are long lasting and great for cutting.

GROWING TIPS: Sow seeds in autumn or spring, making sure they are covered with soil, as they germinate better in darkness. Plant in full sunshine, where it will be happy in most soils, especially those on the dry side.

INDIAN BLANKET
Gaillardia pulchella

As the name suggests, Indian Blanket is brilliantly colourful with its red-and-yellow banded flowers. It's native to the USA, where it commonly grows along roadsides, flowering from June to September.

GROWING TIPS: Sow seeds shallowly in pots or trays and plant in full sunshine, ideally in poor, dry soil.

QUEEN ANNE'S LACE OR **WILD CARROT**
Daucus carota

Wild Carrot might not sound too exciting, but this is a beauty with sturdy, creamy umbrella-like flowers that become structural, filigree baskets as they go over. It's another biennial but loves poor soil and a dry spot, where its deep carrot-like tap root can reach hidden water. It also provides an excellent food source for many bees, hoverflies and beetles. In the USA, it's proved a problem in some states where it has been all too successful and self-seeding, so it might be best avoided there.

GROWING TIPS: Sow seeds in autumn, as they need a period of cold to get the seed ready to germinate.

EVENING PRIMROSE
Oenothera biennis

As its Latin name suggests, this is another biennial, but one that self-seeds so freely that it always seems to be in flower. It's a great choice for dryer soils and poor ground, where it thrives, even seeding beside railway tracks. You'll spot this US native almost everywhere in Europe too, and there's no mistaking those spikes of lemon yellow, open flowers.

GROWING TIPS: Sow seeds in late autumn or early spring, in pots or directly into the ground. If growing in pots, make sure you plant them out in their first year, when they are a rosette of leaves, as this tall plant needs time to develop a long tap root into the ground.

OTHER ANNUAL WILDFLOWERS THAT ARE EASY TO GROW

- **FLAX** *Linum*
- **FORGET-ME-NOT** *Myosotis*
- **COSMOS**
- **POT MARIGOLD** *Calendula*
- **BORAGE**
- **TEASEL** *Dipsacus*
- **LARKSPUR** *Consolida*
- **ZINNIA**
- **CORN MARIGOLD** *Glebionis*
- **SUNFLOWER** *Helianthus*

'As I wander'd the forest,
The green leaves among,
I heard a Wild Flower
Singing a Song.'

WILLIAM BLAKE

Top left, clockwise: Forget-Me-Not, Cosmos,
Flax, Teasel, Pot Marigold, Borage

WILDFLOWER FOLKLORE

CUCKOO FLOWER
Cardamine pratensis

Cuckoo Flower might not sound that prepossessing a wildflower until you realise that its name came about because it was believed to herald the first cuckoo of spring. One of my favourite spring wildflowers, this charming little plant appears in late spring and grows in damp, grassy meadows and bogs, its petals tinted pink or soft mauve. It's also known by the names 'Lady's Smock', 'Milkmaid' and 'May Flower', and is linked with the revels of May, when 'hedge witches' used various parts of the plant for love potions and fertility spells – as well as the opposite: charms intended to keep love and fertility at bay.

Cuckoo Flower was believed to be sacred to fairies, hence another of its names, 'Fairy Flower'. It was deemed bad luck to bring it indoors, probably because it was thought to encourage fairies into your home. The name 'Lady's Smock', while ostensibly describing the shape of the flowers, was also said to reflect its resemblance to the garments of frolicking lovers strewn about the meadow in springtime.

One of the many great things about the cuckoo flower rooted in fact rather than folklore is that it is also a key food plant for the Orange-tip butterfly, another harbinger of spring.

BIRDS AND MISTLETOE

Mistletoe is rather different from your average common-or-garden plant. Not only is it completely reliant on birds to spread its seed, but it is often found hanging in trees in great balls, as it's a very successful parasite, sometimes colonising entire copses. Technically, mistletoe is a hemi-parasite, which means it makes some of its energy itself through photosynthesis, with the rest coming from the host plant.

Mistletoe is brilliantly adaptive, having evolved into more than 1,000 species that are specific to hosts as diverse as pine trees and cacti, although the ones we usually spot are on deciduous trees, such as oak and apple.

Another clever thing about mistletoe is that its pale, translucent berries are incredibly sticky – and they need to be, because they only stand a chance of germinating on a tree; they haven't a hope on the ground. This is where the birds come in: all those different mistletoe species attract different birds to eat them in different countries. In the USA, the desert bird Phainopepla relies on mistletoe as its main winter food source, spreading the plant through the acacia and mesquite trees of the Sonoran Desert. In the UK, it's often blackcaps and thrushes, particularly Mistle Thrushes, that you'll see feasting on the fruits, which the plant cleverly produces in winter when there is little other food about. The birds find their beaks covered with the berries' sticky glaze, which they scrape off onto a branch, depositing the mistletoe seed exactly where it wants to be – on another tree.

If that fails, the mistletoe has a backup plan – wait for the berry to pass through the bird's gut and be pooped out, with its ready-made glue, on a handy twig or branch. That's how mistletoe derived its lovely name: from the rather less-lovely Anglo-Saxon word for dung, 'mistel', and the word 'tan' for twig, evolving into mistletoe over time.

CHAPTER THREE

THE LIFE OF YOUR LAWN

Y ou might think of your lawn as simply a green tablecloth that sets off the surrounding borders, or a football pitch, or somewhere to sunbathe, but there's a lot more going on that's not obvious. Next time you're lying in the sun, take a good look at what is happening in that dense thicket of grassy stems. I guarantee there will be a bustle of activity: ants, woodlice, spiders and beetles all using the lawn for cover, feeding and gathering nesting material.

Added to that, your lawn probably contains a lot more than just grass. Unless you're devoted to using weed and moss killers, it will undoubtedly have clumps of bright little daisy flowers popping up almost as soon as you've mown it. The darker, damper edges in the shade will be bright green with moss and the more you leave off weed killing, the more variety there will be.

Why is that so important? Just think of a manicured, weed-free lawn as a desert. It's a monoculture, which takes a lot of effort and chemicals to keep in its pristine, purely grass, state. It is equally a desert for wildlife, partly because the chemical treatments necessary to maintain it are highly detrimental to wild creatures, but also because mown grass produces no flowers, so no nectar or pollen for insects, no seeds for birds and mice and no predators preying on the smaller creatures. A desert. Our lawns take up a massive amount of the space in our gardens, so the more wildflowers they contain, the more they attract, feed and provide habitats and homes for wildlife. Your lawn is a fantastic resource for wild creatures – as long as you stop killing weeds, adding fertiliser and mowing it super short. Stop using chemicals and raise the height of your lawnmower, and the wildflowers will come by themselves. Letting wildflowers such as daisies and clover come back into your lawn does wonders for the wildlife of your garden – and won't do any harm to the lawn either. In fact, wildflowers are often far more resilient to periods of drought than grass species, so some daisies and clover will keep your lawn looking green when pure grass lawns are brown and parched. It may not be a golf-green-perfect lawn any more, but it will still be short and sturdy enough for a game of football.

TOP LAWN WILDFLOWERS TO ENCOURAGE

RED CLOVER
Trifolium pratense

You'll spot clover's characteristic trefoil leaves in garden lawns, hedgerows, farm fields and meadows all over. Red clover is the bigger and bolder of the clovers, with pink-red, nectar-rich flowers appearing from spring until autumn when they get the chance to bloom. It's worth letting them flower in your lawn as they attract lots of different bees, including honey bees, red-tailed bumblebees and common carder bees.

WHITE CLOVER
Trifolium repens

Have you ever found a lucky four-leafed clover? As common as the red clover, white clover is just as popular with wildlife and just as easy to spot with its white-marked, classic trefoil leaves. Wood mice collect their leaves and use them to mark their routes. They are also a food source for many animals, from small rodents to deer. Like other clovers, white clover is a member of the pea family and has the same nitrogen-fixing nodules on its roots, helping it to stay lush and green even in drought periods. As for four-leafed clovers, they do exist and, in fact, there are clover farms in the USA that specialize in growing them to harvest and sell as good-luck charms.

DAISY
Bellis perennis

You probably have a few daisies in your lawn already – they are one of the most common and easiest to recognize of all wildflowers. Given a little sunshine, they flower practically all year round, and their densely packed rosettes of leaves gradually spread across the lawn, smothering the grass as they grow. Daisies love the shorter grass of a lawn, often flowering just beneath the mower height of cut, producing the dainty little flowers once called 'day's eyes'. Don't you remember the joy of making daisy chains when you were little? Or the 'he loves me, he loves me not' game of plucking away single daisy petals until your answer becomes clear?

BIRD'S-FOOT TREFOIL
Lotus corniculatus

It's easy to miss the dainty bird's-foot trefoil until it blooms, when its bright yellow little flowers and red buds earn it the common name of 'Eggs and Bacon'. Another of its common names is the unforgettable 'Granny's Toenails', which describes its clawed seedpods rather well. While it's slower to establish than some lawn flowers, once you have it, it seeds and spreads happily – which is great as it's an important food plant for several butterflies, including some that are regarded as in peril.

SELFHEAL
Prunella vulgaris

You will barely notice the creeping, dark green leaves of selfheal until it flowers, when its short, purple-blue spikes make it look more like a garden plant. As its name suggests, selfheal was used in herbal medicines to cure everything from wounds to a sore throat, and it grows anywhere from roadside verges to woodland and untreated lawns. To get it to flower, you have to stop mowing for a few weeks, but its flowers are lovely and provide an important source of nectar for bees and wasps.

YARROW
Achillea millefolium

The distinctive feathery leaves of yarrow are unmistakeable, even without the flowers, which are regularly cut off by mowing. Yarrow is a real survivor, with its deep, water-gathering tap roots allowing it to thrive in all sorts of unwelcoming situations, such as seaside grassland. Given a chance, its elegant pink and white flower heads spring up from its dense rosettes of feathery leaves. That elegance and persistence has made yarrow a plant that gardeners have developed into a range of attractive border plants, such as the *Achillea* 'Tutti Frutti' series.

DANDELION
Taraxacum officinale

The common dandelion gets such a bad press from
gardeners and, with its characteristic deep tap roots,
is a nuisance to weed out if you don't catch it when
small. But it's an undoubted winner with wildlife,
flowering prolifically and early in the season, providing
an essential food source for pollinators. Children, too,
love playing dandelion 'clocks' – counting the time as
they blow the seeds off the puffy seed heads and watch
them float away…

THREE WAYS TO MAKE A FLOWERING LAWN

In late winter and early spring, use a springbok rake to scarify or scratch up the lawn so that you can see the bare soil beneath in some patches. Sow a wildflower mix or individual species into these areas.

Plant plugs or small pots of wildflowers into your lawn in spring. These can be ones you've bought – there are lots available on mail order (see chapter 8) – or ones you've grown yourself. Planting into a localized area makes it easier to water the young plants if the weather turns dry, though you can also see how the plants colonise the wider lawn over the next few seasons.

If you're starting a lawn from scratch on a bare patch of soil, it pays to sow with a flowering lawn mix rather than a plain mix of just grass species. These include species that flower low and can be mown, and that knit together surprisingly quickly. There's no need to remove the topsoil to sow these wildflower mixes.

WHAT CAN YOU EXPECT TO SEE?

Lawns, even regularly mown ones, provide a home for all sorts of wildlife. You might see anything from insects to frogs, newts, hedgehogs and even foxes on your lawn. Starting from the base layer, where soil meets grass, you'll find ants, woodlice, spiders and beetles. Dig a little deeper and there are earthworms, insect larvae, such as wireworms and leatherjackets, and all sorts of tiny creatures living in the soil. Short grass is a magnet for insect-eating birds such as starlings, blackbirds, robins and song thrushes, while longer grass offers shelter and egg-laying opportunities to insects, attracting birds and other wildlife that prey on them. Let your lawn flowers bloom, and the clover will bring in bees, while the seeds from the grasses, plantains and dandelions will attract hungry birds and mice.

Less welcome are the holes that foxes, badgers and moles dig in the lawn when searching for food, but I think the joy of seeing a fox flitting through your garden makes any damage worthwhile.

LOOK OUT FOR...

BLACK GARDEN ANTS

These are your classic garden ants that nest in the soil, especially in lawns or at the base of walls. Their busy colonies are a joy to watch, with the black or dark brown ants going about their business untiringly until, in high summer, the winged ants emerge all at once, filling the air in a swarm as they mate.

VIOLET GROUND BEETLES

This beetle is something of a beauty with is shiny wing cases edged in deep violet. It's also a great friend to the gardener, as it's a lively hunter – even its larvae devour slugs, worms and other insects.

CRANEFLIES

The 'daddy-long-legs' is a common sight in late summer and, as fragile as the adults are, their larvae are the chunky leatherjackets that live in the soil layer of lawns, eating the roots, and providing a good meal for lively birds.

CHAFERS

There are several different kinds of chafer beetle or May bug, including the beautiful metallic Rose Chafer, but all are great zeppelins, buzzing about the garden in ungainly fashion in May or June, feeding in trees and shrubs. They lay their eggs in the lawn where their fat grubs make a marvellous meal for birds.

MINING BEES

If you're lucky, you might spot a gently moving swarm of bees emerging from their holes in your lawn in spring. These Mining Bees are the gentlest of bees and it's a joy to behold their short spring awakening, before they're off and about their business for the summer. They often return to the same dry lawn areas to nest for winter year after year.

WILDFLOWER FOLKLORE

BUTTERCUPS

Wildflower meadows wouldn't be the same without the sunshine flowers of the meadow buttercup. Indeed, in the folk tradition of the western UK, buttercups are associated with the sun, yellow butter and the dairy. On May Day, farmers traditionally rubbed the udders of their cows with buttercup flowers to increase the quantity and richness of their milk. This was also thought to protect the cows from theft by fairies, who were always eager to improve their herds of fairy cattle by interbreeding with cows from mortal fields.

One of the best folk tales related to cows, buttercups and fairies tells of a miser who was punished for not sharing his money with the fairies when crossing their meadow one day. The angry fairies poked a hole in his bag, allowing his gold coins to fall to the ground, where the fairies turned them into golden yellow flowers so he wouldn't notice their trick.

Another story tells of a farmer who believed that grazing his cow on buttercup flowers rather than just grass gave it the sweetest milk of any of the neighbouring farmers' cows. This is pure folklore as buttercups have an acrid taste and would make both cows and humans ill if ingested. It's because the cows avoid eating the buttercups that our fields remain full of these sunshine flowers.

MONARCH BUTTERFLIES AND MILKWEED

Monarch butterflies and their epic, generation-spanning migration from Canada to Mexico are one of the wonders of the natural world. But their journey wouldn't be possible without milkweed, an unprepossessing wildflower that is everything to the Monarch butterfly.

Monarch butterflies feed on the nectar of milkweed, along with a number of other wildflowers, transferring pollen as they go and helping the milkweed to reproduce. But it's as a food plant for caterpillars that milkweed is vital. Adult Monarchs lay their eggs singly on the leaves of milkweed plants and once those caterpillars hatch nothing but milkweed will do as food, with each caterpillar chomping through 20 or so leaves before reaching the pupal stage.

Fortunately there are over 100 different milkweed species and they grow happily in a range of conditions. The bad news is that, like many wild plants, milkweed is susceptible to habitat loss and agricultural chemicals, which makes growing wildflowers in your garden all the more important.

CHAPTER FOUR

HOW TO MAKE
A MEADOW

L etting your lawn grow a little is a good start but you can go one step further if you have the space and enthusiasm. Making a meadow can be very straightforward or a longer process, depending on how you set about it. Whichever way you choose, creating a meadow from a bare patch of ground or a boring lawn is an incredibly joyful process, one of evolution and hope, where you can watch the flora you plant establish itself, and the fauna, seemingly arriving from nowhere, make itself at home.

A meadow doesn't need to be big – swathes of flowers are fab if you have acres of garden, but even a tiny, postage-stamp meadow will do wonders for wildlife. Urban meadows are especially important as wildflowers are hard to come by in towns and cities, except in pavements cracks, although parks are becoming increasingly more 'wild' as local authorities embrace a more holistic approach to managing their green spaces. But parks are few and far between, and urban gardens link together to form green chains or corridors, which makes your patch of wildflowers a little oasis for smaller wildlife, such as insects, invertebrates, and the frogs, toads, hedgehogs and larger mammals like foxes that feed on them.

Don't worry how big or small your meadow is – the crucial thing is to have one. Whether it's a border given over to meadow flowers, a patch by the shed or under the hedge where you establish some shade-loving meadow plants, or a section of lawn allowed to grow longer and wilder until late summer, it will make a difference.

WHAT IS A MEADOW?

Traditionally, a meadow is a natural evolution of grasses and wildflowers that has evolved undisturbed over decades or longer, managed with regular, seasonal cutting for hay and grazing by animals. Nowadays, we tend to refer to a meadow as a broader category comprising large drifts of wildflowers, with or without grasses. Traditional meadows were often filled with perennial species that would flower year after year, while modern meadows can be a perennial mixture or an annual mix that's re-sown each year. Annual mixes give you the opportunity to add variety to your garden every year – and they're also a great deal easier to manage than a perennial meadow. If you're not sure about a meadow at all, just try sowing an annual mix in a border or bare patch and have some fun.

THE QUICK WAY TO MAKE A MEADOW

You might think that the quickest way to make a meadow is to just let your lawn grow and see what appears, but chances are you'll only get a lot of grass and perhaps some clover at first. Only after several years will other species start to pop up. In that time, you'll likely lose heart, get fed up with the garden looking a mess and decide to go back to mowing the grass. Rather than lose enthusiasm, start by keeping your lawn mown, but create wildflower 'borders', so that your lawn merges into a wildflower meadow. Using annual wildflower mixes gives you just one season of wildflowers, so you haven't taken too much of a plunge. You can always get into a more permanent, perennial meadow later as you gain confidence.

The ideal way to create a meadow swiftly and simply is by starting with bare ground, weeded, tilled and prepared as if ready for sowing a lawn. That is straightforward if the area is small, as it can easily be prepared by hand. If you're looking at reseeding a larger area, the preparation will be more involved, perhaps involving machinery and manpower.

Sowing a perennial meadow from scratch requires very thorough soil preparation. It's vital to get this as good as possible as the plants will be there for a long time. All the persistent weeds such as nettles, brambles and docks need to be removed and you might even need to take off some of the topsoil. Weeds like these are often indicators of too rich a soil, where the grasses will thrive but the wildflowers will not.

THE LONG WAY

The long way of making a meadow is a process of gradual improvement that allows you to really get to know your meadow. It's a bit like slow cooking, slow TV and all those slow movements – the journey is part of the whole.

In my opinion, this slower method is by far the most rewarding way of making a meadow – provided you have the time and patience – as well as the most traditional, involving gently evolving an interwoven network of species. It's a hark back to the hay meadows that until recently made up a large swathe of agricultural land.

There are few things more beautiful than a traditional hay meadow in June. As well as all the grasses that are growing tall and flowering themselves, it's also full of flowers ranging from several species of Meadow Cranesbill to Oxeye Daisies, buttercups, Lady's Bedstraw…the list goes on. A good hay meadow can be home to as many as 100 different species of plant, and goodness knows how many different insects and animals.

Hay meadows rely on a specific type of management that has been going on for hundreds of years. This involves allowing the grasses to get tall, before cutting them for hay, then grazing the meadow for the remainder of the season. This stops any one plant gaining dominance and keeps it gloriously diverse. But with the rise of silage and chemical controls, Europe's hay meadows are not the common sight they once were, meaning anything that gardeners can do to preserve this precious ecological evolution is a good thing.

Creating a hay meadow involves introducing these species into the mix of grasses, reducing the vigour of the competing grasses, then cutting and mowing the meadow as if you were making hay, and grazing the sward afterwards. A low impact way to make your lawn more of a meadow is to scarify a section with a rake, scratching out the grass 'thatch' until you can see the soil surface, then scattering wildflower seed into these exposed patches. This is a bit hit-and-miss as the germinating wildflowers have to compete with the grass, but it's a good way to introduce vigorous plants such as Yellow Rattle (*Rhinanthus minor*), which is a meadow essential. This semi-parasitic plant competes wonderfully with grass, slowing down its growth and allowing other wildflowers to establish.

ENJOYING YOUR MEADOW

Meadows look great right the way through spring and summer, but their peak is often in late June and July, just when we're getting out into the garden to enjoy the sun. Make sure you mow paths and clearings into your meadow so you can get in among the flowers and insects. Lying on a blanket listening to the hum of bees, the gentle swish of grass stems in the breeze, and the sound of seedpods cracking is a delight, even in the smallest garden. Meadows are alive with the movement of flowers and grasses, bees, butterflies and moths. Birds flit down to pick off insects, while hoverflies linger above the flowers and the fresh scent of pollen, crushed grass and meadow herbs fills the summer air.

KEY EUROPEAN MEADOW WILDFLOWERS

YELLOW RATTLE
Rhinanthus minor
This pretty little flower looks innocent, but it's an effective parasitic plant that attaches itself to the roots of rampant grasses, weakening their growth and so assisting other, less competitive wildflowers.

FIELD SCABIOUS
Knautia arvensis
These attractive, pin-cushion flowers appear in midsummer and keep on coming, studding your meadow or border with the softest lilac shades and attracting bees and butterflies in droves.

KNAPWEED
Centaurea scabiosa
Bees and butterflies also love these pretty 'raggedy' flowers in rich purple-pink on sturdy stems.

LADY'S BEDSTRAW

Galium verum

These little flowers add a froth and fragrance to the meadow that is unmistakeable in July and August. Their name derives from the fact that these scented flowers were thought to repel fleas and so were used to stuff mattresses.

PLANTAIN

Plantago

There are several species of plantain and all are good in meadows, where they can produce their characteristic spear-shaped flowers, which attract hoverflies, moths and smaller butterfly species. The seeds are also good for birds.

MEADOW GRASSES

CRESTED DOG'S TAIL
Cynosurus cristatus

A pretty grass with flattened flower
spikes on sturdy stems. These stems
were traditionally used to make
straw hats.

YORKSHIRE FOG
Holcus lanatus

A major part of hay meadows, this
grass is a true beauty when it flowers,
producing a mist of pink-tinged,
soft flowers above grey, slightly
furred leaves.

COMMON BENT
Agrostis capillaris

This drought-tolerant grass species
is incredibly dainty, fine-leaved and
has open, airy flowers that give it it's
common name of browntop bent.

QUAKING GRASS
Briza media

This is the prettiest grass and one
that is well worth a place in the border
in its own right. Easy to grow from
seed, it will self-seed freely on poor,
dry soils, but fades away if the
ground is too rich or fertilised.

COCK'S-FOOT
Dactylis glomerata

Robust, tussocky and vigorous, this
is a grass for larger meadows.

WHAT TO SPOT IN YOUR MEADOW

Meadow Brown Butterfly

By far the most common grassland butterfly in the UK, the Meadow Brown might look rather plain, but it's a delight to spot fluttering over your meadow as it feeds on the grass flowers and lays her eggs among them. Many other butterflies, such as Marbled Whites and Large Skippers, also frequent meadow flowers and grasses.

Day-flying Moths

There are several species of day-flying moths, which you are more likely to see than their nocturnal cousins. The spectacular Burnet moth loves meadow plants, such as knapweed, and will often live its entire life in one single meadow. Another eye-catching day moth is the Mother Shipton moth, named after a famous Yorkshire witch because its spectacular wing markings resemble a witch's face.

Grasshoppers

The chirruping of grasshoppers is a common sound in grassland in July. The ones you're likely to see are the Meadow Grasshopper and the Common Green.

White-tailed Bumblebee

You'll see all sorts of bees buzzing over a meadow looking for nectar and pollen, but bumblebees are the easiest ones to spot and identify. They'll often nest in small animal burrows around the edges of a meadow.

Goldfinches

With all the insect life and seeds on offer, it's no surprise that birds are attracted to meadows. Goldfinches are possibly the most eye-catching, and both European and American varieties, although completely different species, share colourful plumage and a penchant for thistle, knapweed, dandelion and teasel seeds.

WILDFLOWER FOLKLORE

VIOLETS

Violets might be small but they're sure to be noticed.
They have a habit of popping up in all sorts of
places, from woodland edges and clearings to garden
borders. Violets are also hugely important for fritillary
butterflies. They are food plants for the caterpillars of
four different fritillary species, with the adult butterflies
deliberately laying their eggs on tree trunks close to
Dog Violets.

The dainty little violet is one of the earliest wildflowers
to bloom, and although they're tiny, their rich blue-
purple does catch the eye. They've been cultivated since
medieval times, used as strewing herbs for scenting
rooms and Shakespeare mentions them frequently
in his works. The folk stories abound, from carrying
violets to ward off evil spirits and strewing them in
baby cradles to provide protection, to giving them
as tokens of good luck and scattering them in bridal
chambers to bring good fortune to the new couple.

Apparently, if you dream of violets, you'll come into a fortune or, alternatively, you'll marry someone younger than yourself. Another belief is that you can only smell the flowers once – which is part based on truth, as violet's scent contains ionine, a compound that affects your sense of smell, deadening it for a short period of time.

Violets were also the emblem of Napoleon Bonaparte, who gave them to Josephine, and told his followers that he would return from exile on Elba when the violets bloomed in the spring. It became a way of identifying his friends, with people asking: "Do you like violets?" and if the answer was yes, it meant you were a loyal supporter. According to historians, the wearing of violets was regarded as seditious after the Battle of Waterloo. A little flower with a big back story.

NATURAL FRIENDSHIPS

ANTS AND WHAT
THEY DO FOR PLANTS

Ants are always busy doing something, and a lot of what they do, while benefitting their colony, is also hugely beneficial to plants. Much of their activity leads to the propagation and spread of plants throughout the garden and in the wild too. In fact, ants disperse more than 30 per cent of the spring-flowering herbaceous plants in eastern North America.

These ant-plants, properly called Myrmecophytes, share a mutualistic relationship with ants. This is when two organisms of different species each benefit from the activity of the other, and those interactions are incredibly diverse. Some 11,000 species of flowering plants produce special seed appendages that give the ants food in exchange for dispersing their seeds. Around 4,000 species have minute pockets of nectar on the leaves or stems, known as extra-floral nectaries, while another 700 or so offer homes for ants in their stems. These are called domatia and the resident ants provide the plants with defence against plant-eating animals.

My favourite example is the little cyclamen species. Once the flowers have finished, they produce pods at the ends of the stems, which then curl and descend to the ground as the seeds within the pod ripen. The ants are then drawn to the protein-rich substance attached to the seed, which they carry back to their nest, discarding the seed afterwards a good distance away from the parent plant. New cyclamen plants can then grow happily in its new spot, the ants will have food for years to come and the whole cycle continues.

CHAPTER FIVE

TEN THINGS TO KNOW ABOUT WILDFLOWERS

Humans disrupting nature is nothing new. We have been interfering with wild flora ever since prehistoric times. Once we learned to make fires, for instance, we inevitably burned off natural vegetation, allowing more aggressive species, perhaps from other areas, to take root.

But the 'arrival' of wildflowers – that is their identification and naming – really begins with the Greeks and Romans, as so many things are. Around the fourth century BC, the 'Father of Botany', Theophrastus, a student of Aristotle, was in charge of the Athens botanical and medicinal gardens, where he studied and named 500 separate plants. Later, Roman scholars studied the development of ornamental and wild-growing plants, famously exporting grapevines, figs and garlic across the Empire, as well as herbs such as mint, rosemary and basil. They also introduced some less-welcome additions such as ground elder, which they may have loved as a vegetable but is now a nuisance weed to many gardeners.

2 **We've been growing poppies forever.** They have been found in Egyptian tombs, and Egyptian physicians believed the seeds relieved pain, while the Ancient Greeks associated poppies with fertility and abundance. There is also evidence that they were grown as ornamental plants in Mesopotamia from 5000 BC.

Poppies are highly symbolic, representing everything from resurrection and eternal life, to restful sleep and the remembrance of those fallen in wars. There's even a section in *The Wonderful Wizard of Oz* where Dorothy and Toto succumb to sleep in a poppy field. In that case, the poppies are somewhat drugging, more reminiscent of the Opium Poppy, *Papaver somniferum*.

3 **Over one third of the world's food crops rely on insects to pollinate them.** Without them, we'd have to pollinate fruit and vegetables by hand or artificially, which is virtually impossible.

But think of wildflowers and you immediately think of their value to pollinators. Wildflowers provide bees, butterflies, hoverflies and other insects with food throughout the year. On a single summer's day, one acre of wildflower meadow can contain something like three million flowers. Those flowers produce one kilo of nectar sugar – enough to support close to 96,000 honey bees each day.

4 **Sunflowers have been used to soak up nuclear radiation.** After the Chernobyl and Fukushima disasters, sunflowers were planted in contaminated areas where their roots extracted radioactive toxins such as lead, arsenic and uranium from contaminated soil.

Sunflowers are native to the Americas, where the Incas believed they were the physical manifestation of the sun god. Sunflowers also hold a key place in Native American cultures as they were used widely for food, oil, in medical preparations, and for creating dyes and body paints. The tallest sunflower ever grown reached the colossal height of 9.17m (30ft 1in) tall.

5 **If you want to be blown away by the sheer power of wildflowers, the Californian deserts are among the best places to see a 'superbloom'.** Every decade or so, the Mojave Desert and the Carrizo Plain play host to an explosion of wildflowers. This spectacular phenomenon, which sees the hills and deserts clothed with a brilliant patchwork of wildflowers all blooming at once, happens only when conditions coincide perfectly. First, the season needs to have been sufficiently dry for grasses to have trouble establishing. Next, there must have been enough rain in the autumn to penetrate deep into the soil where the wildflower seeds lie dormant. After this, it takes a perfect coming together of sufficient moisture, cloud cover to shield the germinating seeds from the sun and severe cold at night, and the desert winds abating for a superbloom to occur.

6 Vincent Van Gogh's 'Yellow Period' – think of his famous Sunflowers – may have been influenced by foxglove or digitalis therapy, which was used at the time to control seizures. The common foxglove, *Digitalis purpurea*, is widely used in medicine today, and is cultivated commercially for the drug digitalis, which helps stimulate the heart. However, back in Van Gogh's day, overuse of digitalis resulted in nausea, vomiting and diarrhoea as well as xanthopsia – a yellowing of the vision – and the appearance of blurred outlines and halos, which all seem reminiscent of his work. Interestingly, a steroid called Digoxigenin or DIG, which is used for detecting RNA and DNA, is only found in the flowers and leaves of *Digitalis purpurea* and two other species of foxglove.

7 The ancients knew a lot more about plants and their properties than we do – but we're catching up. Flowering plants provide almost 25 per cent of the basic ingredients for modern drugs, with that figure rising closer to 80 per cent when it comes to antibiotics, cardiovascular, immunotherapy and anti-cancer drugs, and there are thousands of plants yet to be studied.

Some are more obvious than others – think of echinacea, mint and garlic – while others have to be broken down into specific compounds to prove effective. Aspirin was originally derived from willow bark, although nowadays it's synthesized. The key ingredient in aspirin is salicylic acid – the willow's Latin name is *Salix* – which is widely used for reducing the risk of heart attacks, alleviating risk of thrombosis, and may even have cancer-fighting properties. There's a lot still to discover, but every time you take an aspirin for a headache, you're following in the footsteps of the Ancient Egyptians, who used to chew the willow bark twigs for the same purpose.

8 **What is a true native wildflower?** Many wildflowers are relatively recent introductions, brought by people into fresh countries either by accident or intentionally as a crop or garden plant. For example, Oxeye Daisy, *Leucanthemum vulgare*, are a firmly established wildflower in all 50 US states, but it first arrived in the USA in sacks of seed brought by colonists. In the UK, the beloved Snowdrop, *Galanthus nivalis*, a regular fixture of Christmas cards and calendars, is often considered a native, but its first known cultivation was in 1597, and it was only recorded in the wild as a naturalised plant in 1778 – and that was just in a couple of areas. Since then, it has spread into almost every corner of the UK, either by self-seeding or by people planting it in their gardens because they love it so much, and then it self-seeds from there.

9 **The Fitzgerald River National Park in Western Australia probably takes the prize for the spot to see the most wildflower species at any one time.** This gigantic park covers over a thousand square miles (3,000 square kilometres) and boasts 12,000 wildflowers species, 60 per cent of which are native.

If it's orchids that take your fancy, head to the Dordogne region of France. From March to July, the area is the place to see nearly 50 species of wild orchid, including Fly, Pyramidal and Bird's Nest orchids in their hundreds.

Crested Butte, on the eastern plains of Colorado, is one of the best – and earliest – places to see wildflowers in the USA. Many start to flower there in April and May, while the western Rockies won't be blooming until the summer months. Crested Butte is so famous for its wildflowers that it even hosts a Wildflower Festival, with hikes, talks, photography and art events.

10 **One person's wildflower is another person's pest.**
Some wildflowers have become serious problems,
usually in their non-native states or countries. For
example, take iconic tumbleweed, a feature of every Western
movie ever made. The plant is actually Russian Thistle, *Salsola
tragus*, which made its first American appearance in the 1870s in
South Dakota, probably after arriving in a consignment of grain
from the Russian Empire, and has since spread to every state
except Florida and Alaska.

Some introductions have been deliberate, such as the Spanish
Bluebell, *Hyacinthoides hispanica*, which was brought to the
UK by keen Victorian gardeners but has since escaped to become
a problem plant. At first glance, it is very similar to the native
bluebell, *Hyacinthoides non-scripta*, but where the native is
delicate, dainty and a rich violet-blue, the Spanish Bluebell is
something of a thug, with big leaves, big pale flowers and the
ability to self-seed at an astonishing rate. What's worse is that it
can hybridize with the native bluebell and has the potential to
out-compete and out-grow it in the wild.

That's why it's so important not to take flowers, seeds or bulbs
from the wild when on holiday.

WILDFLOWER FOLKLORE

FOXGLOVE

There's some debate about the origins of the name foxglove, but it does date back to Anglo-Saxon times, so some confusion is understandable. The 'glove' part of the name is deemed to be due to the flowers looking like glove fingers, but the 'fox' part could be a corruption of 'folks', meaning fairy folk. There are hordes of names for this eye-catching plant, ranging from 'Fairy Fingers', 'Ladies' Thimbles', 'Throatwort', 'Flapdock', 'Cow-flop', 'Lionsmouth' and 'Scotch Mercury' to the ominous 'Dead Man's Bells' and 'Witches' Gloves'. In fact, more than 30 are recorded – more than for any other UK wildflower. A rather lovely story has it that foxes would wear the flowers on their paws to make them silent when hunting. The truth is that the name probably came about because foxgloves often grow close to foxes' dens in woods or waste ground.

The folklore of foxgloves, like the plant itself, is also somewhat ambiguous. In folk stories it's sometimes regarded as a healing symbol but it can also have negative and hurtful connotations, which reflect the plant's dual character, as both an agent for healing heart problems and as a potentially fatal poison. The name Dead Man's Bells is an outright warning to steer clear of the plant and its potentially fatal effect, and in many areas folk stories told that picking a foxglove would offend the fairies – in all likelihood a tale designed to prevent children from picking its poisonous flowers. The name 'Witches' Gloves', while sounding fanciful, is, in fact, steeped in history from the days when village 'wise women' were often the only physicians available. Foxglove was used for treating abscesses, boils and open wounds, as well as epilepsy and headaches. It's easy to imagine how difficult it would be to get the dosage correct in those times, which is perhaps why those poor wise women became known as witches.

FOXES AND LARGER MAMMALS

You might think that the relationship between plants and foxes and other larger mammals is strictly one way, in that mammals eat plants. But parent plants are inordinately inventive in making sure they reproduce successfully and spreading their offspring into new territories. Getting eaten by a larger mammal requires the seed to be tough enough to survive the whole digestive process but it does mean it will be deposited, eventually, somewhere fresh with a handy dollop of fertiliser to get started. In fact, the seeds of many plants are reliant on passing through a digestive system to ready them for germination. In the UK, badgers help to spread Yew, *Taxus baccata*, allowing trees to colonise new patches of woodland. The badgers swallow the berries in a gulp, digesting the red pulp and leaving the hard seeds intact to pass through their bodies.

Other plants simply hitchhike, using animals, including us, as vehicles to disperse their seeds. These plants, such as Burdock, *Arctium* sp, and Cleavers or Goosegrass, *Galium aparine*, have developed 'sticky' or prickly seeds specifically designed to attach to the coat of a passing fox or trouser leg or bootlace. These then get deposited far away when the animal scratches or rubs against a tree – or brushes off their boots and trousers.

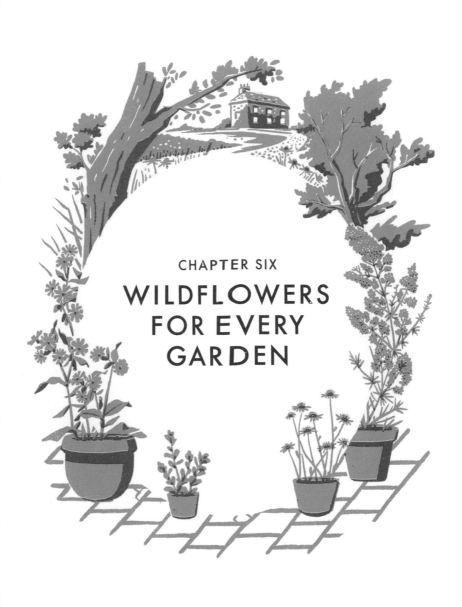

CHAPTER SIX

WILDFLOWERS
FOR EVERY
GARDEN

Wherever your garden is – city or suburb, courtyard or rooftop – there are wildflowers that will thrive in it. Don't worry if you have thin soil or your garden is shady all the time – many wildflowers love sites where ornamental plants might need lots of ground preparation and aftercare. One of the great things about wildflowers is that they're survivors, adapting to prevailing conditions and thriving where many cultivated plants do not.

Choose your plants carefully, taking into account the peculiarities of your garden, and you should get good results. But do remember that these are wildflowers, and by their very nature, not as neat or as showy as many cultivated plants that have been specially bred for compactness and full-on floweriness. The impact of wildflowers in the garden is far more subtle: less about show and more about harmony between plants and wildlife.

SUN WORSHIPPERS

Most wildflowers thrive in the sunshine – just think of sunny meadows – but some are sure-fire winners in sunny spots. If in doubt, check the packet or plant label to be on the safe side. Don't worry if your soil is poor as most of the flowers listed here will be quite happy in it. What's more, many of the flowers on one list can grow equally well in other types of soil, so don't regard these lists as definitive by any means.

FOR HEAVY CLAY SOILS

Cowslip	*Primula veris*
Oxeye Daisy	*Leucanthemum vulgare*
Knapweed	*Centaurea* species
Meadowsweet	*Filipendula ulmaria*
Ribwort Plantain	*Plantago lanceolata*
Field Scabious	*Knautia arvensis*
Selfheal	*Prunella vulgaris*
Poppy	*Papaver rhoeas*
Lady's Bedstraw	*Galium verum*
Salad Burnet	*Sanguisorba minor*

FOR DRY SOILS

St John's Wort	*Hypericum perforatum*
Viper's Bugloss	*Echium vulgare*
Yarrow	*Achillea millefolium*
Field Forget-Me-Not	*Myosotis arvensis*
Oxeye Daisy	*Leucanthemum vulgare*
Wild Carrot	*Daucus carota*
Selfheal	*Prunella vulgaris*
Wild Marjoram	*Origanum vulgare*
Bird's-Foot Trefoil	*Lotus corniculatus*

QUICK-RESULT ANNUALS

Poppy	*Papaver rhoeas*
Cornflower	*Centaurea cyanus*
Corn Chamomile	*Anthemis arvensis*
Corncockle	*Agrostemma githago*
Corn Marigold	*Chrysanthemum segetum*

SHADE LOVERS

Wildflowers can brighten up a shady spot beautifully, adding charm and colour to spaces where other plants wouldn't be happy. Use woodland plants to fill denser shade, but many wildflowers grow well in lighter, dappled shade, so give them a go.

Foxglove *Digitalis purpurea*

The must-have plant for shade, foxglove has unmistakeable stately flowers and self-seeds freely around the garden. It's easy to collect the seeds yourself and sow them exactly where you want.

Selfheal *Prunella vulgaris*

This vigorous little plant often colonizes shady lawns, bravely trying to flower under the mower blades. It's a real survivor, so easy to grow, and a beauty if allowed to bloom with its purple-lipped flowers a magnet for bees and other insects.

Red Campion *Silene dioica*

A lovely garden plant for shade where its flowers seem to glow. Prefers moist, rich soil where it will self-seed happily.

Nettle-Leaved Bellflower *Campanula trachelium*

This campanula is a brilliant bee plant and great for heavier, clay soils and shade.

Cow Parsley *Anthriscus sylvestris*

Happy in part shade, cow parsley self-seeds as much as you let it, colonising dappled dry shade under trees and providing insects with plenty of pollen and nectar from its clouds of white flowers.

OTHER SHADE LOVERS

Hemp Agrimony	*Eupatorium cannabinum*
Angelica	*Angelica* species
Sweet Woodruff	*Galium odoratum*
Sweet Cicely	*Myrrhis odorata*
Wood Avens	*Geum urbanum*
Betony	*Stachys officinalis*
Hedge Garlic	*Alliaria petiolata*
Wild Garlic/Ramsons	*Allium ursinum*

WILDFLOWERS IN POTS AND CONTAINERS

If you only have a little courtyard or rooftop garden, growing wildflowers in pots, window boxes and containers is your best bet. While some deeper-rooted and taller-growing wildflowers don't do well in pots and containers, many are perfect for growing this way. Plenty of wildflowers cope just fine with the dryer, more challenging conditions of containers. Although you still need to water them, they don't mind being a little on the dry side from time to time. Also, most wildflowers love sunshine – great for exposed rooftop gardens –while the ones that don't are brilliant in shade – perfect for basement courtyards and stairwells.

The bigger the container, the more flowers you can pack in, but it's vital to ensure good drainage by raising your pots on 'feet' or bricks. Water regularly, but only when the compost feels dry, and make sure you add some loam or garden soil and grit to your shop-bought compost to keep the mixture open, grainy, and low in nutrients, which is just what wildflowers want.

MY FAVOURITE WILDFLOWERS FOR POTS

Pasqueflower *Pulsatilla vulgaris*

A dainty plant that nevertheless puts on a big show in spring with its stunning, silky, purple flowers followed by feathery seed heads. Once the flowers finish, the ferny foliage is also a delight. But don't disturb it once planted, as it resents being moved.

Field Scabious *Knautia arvensis*

This is perfect for larger pots and containers with its tall, pin-cushion flowers in a lovely shade of mauve. The soft foliage is also attractive and the flowers keep on coming if you deadhead regularly.

Sweet Woodruff *Galium odoratum*

This might be small and dainty, but it is wonderfully charming in containers. The fresh foliage is a vivid shade of green and the little white flowers shine out from shady, dark corners.

Fox and Cubs *Pilosella aurantiaca*

These rich, burnt-orange flowers look wonderful studded through a mix of grasses and wildflowers in a large container.

Wild Marjoram and Thyme *Origanum vulgare* **and** *Thymus* **species**

For urban pots and containers, you can't go wrong with wild herbs. Not only are they easy to grow and brilliant for pollinating insects, but they're also great to have to hand for cooking.

There's a whole host to choose from, including many different forms of marjoram and thyme.

MORE PLANTS FOR POTS AND CONTAINERS

LOW GROWING

Bird's-Foot Trefoil	*Lotus corniculatus*
Dog Violet	*Viola canina*
Wild Strawberry	*Fragaria vesca*
Primrose	*Primula vulgaris*
Red Clover	*Trifolium pratense*
Harebell	*Campanula rotundifolia*

TALLER GROWING

Spiked Speedwell	*Veronica spicata*
Greater Knapweed	*Centaurea scabiosa*
Red Campion	*Silene dioica*
Toadflax	*Linaria vulgaris*
Purple Toadflax	*Linaria purpurea*

ANNUALS

Poppy	*Papaver rhoeas*
Cornflower	*Centaurea cyanus*

BULBS

Snowdrop	*Galanthus nivalis*
Wild Daffodil	*Narcissus pseudonarcissus*
Snake's Head Fritillary	*Fritillaria meleagris*

WILDFLOWERS BY US REGION

The climate varies enormously across the USA. Many wildflowers grow in more than one region, but the following is a short list of some that do well in particular areas.

NORTHEAST

Red Columbine	*Aquilegia canadensis*
Swamp Milkweed	*Asclepias incarnata*
Butterfly Weed	*Asclepias tuberosa*
New England Aster	*Symphyotrichum novae-angliae*
Lanceleaf Coreopsis	*Coreopsis lanceolata*
Joe Pye Weed	*Eutrochium purpureum*
Indian Blanket	*Gaillardia pulchella*
Oxeye Sunflower	*Heliopsis helianthoides*
Blazing Star	*Liatris spicata*
Wild Lupine	*Lupinus perennis*
Wild Bergamot	*Monarda fistulosa*
Evening Primrose	*Oenothera biennis*
Black-Eyed Susan	*Rudbeckia hirta*

SOUTHEAST

Butterfly Weed	*Asclepias tuberosa*
Lanceleaf Coreopsis	*Coreopsis lanceolata*
Plains Coreopsis	*Coreopsis tinctoria*
Purple Coneflower	*Echinacea purpurea*
Indian Blanket	*Gaillardia pulchella*
Blazing Star	*Liatris spicata*

Wild Lupine	*Lupinus perennis*
Lemon Beebalm	*Monarda citriodora*
Mexican Hat	*Ratibida columnifera*
Black-Eyed Susan	*Rudbeckia hirta*

MIDWEST

Red Columbine	*Aquilegia canadensis*
Butterfly Weed	*Asclepias tuberosa*
Blazing Star	*Liatris spicata*
Blue False Indigo	*Baptisia australis*
New England Aster	*Symphyotrichum novae-angliae*
Tall Tickseed	*Coreopsis tripteris*
Purple Coneflower	*Echinacea purpurea*
Joe Pye Weed	*Eupatorium maculatum*
Oxeye Sunflower	*Heliopsis helianthoides*
Wild Lupine	*Lupinus perennis*
Black-Eyed Susan	*Rudbeckia hirta*
Zigzag Goldenrod	*Solidago flexicaulis*

SOUTHWEST

Plains Coreopsis	*Coreopsis tinctoria*
Desert Marigold	*Baileya multiradiata*
Tahoka Daisy	*Machaeranthera tanacetifolia*
California Poppy	*Eschscholzia californica*
Indian Blanket	*Gaillardia pulchella*
Blazing Star	*Liatris spicata*

Blue Flax	*Linum perenne*
Arizona Lupine	*Lupinus arizonicus*
Evening Primrose	*Oenothera biennis*
California Bluebell	*Phacelia minor*
Mexican Hat	*Ratibida columnifera*
Bird's Eyes	*Gilia tricolor*
Five Spot	*Nemophila maculata*

WESTERN

Colorado Blue Columbine	*Aquilegia coerulea*
Smooth Aster	*Symphyotrichum laeve*
Tahoka Daisy	*Machaeranthera tanacetifolia*
Rocky Mountain Bee Plant	*Cleome serrulata*
Plains Coreopsis	*Coreopsis tinctoria*
Showy Fleabane	*Erigeron speciosus*
Indian Blanket	*Gaillardia pulchella*
Globe Gilia	*Gilia capitata*
Blue Flax	*Linum perenne*
Evening Primrose	*Oenothera biennis*
Mexican Hat	*Ratibida columnifera*
Black-Eyed Susan	*Rudbeckia hirta*

PACIFIC NORTHWEST

Plains Coreopsis	*Coreopsis tinctoria*
California Poppy	*Eschscholzia californica*
Globe Gilia	*Gilia capitata*

Blue Flax	*Linum perenne*
Large-Leaved Lupine	*Lupinus polyphyllus*
Blazing Star	*Liatris spicata*
Five Spot	*Nemophila maculata*
Evening Primrose	*Oenothera biennis*
Baby Blue Eyes	*Nemophila menziesii*
California Bluebell	*Phacelia minor*

FLOWER CRAB SPIDERS

Look carefully under a flower and you might just spot a Flower Crab Spider lying in wait for prey. There are 27 species of crab spider in the UK, and their name comes from their strong, pincer-like front legs and the fact they can run sideways. Not all are as striking as the Flower Crab Spider, however.

These clever little arachnids are cunning hunters. Unlike many spiders, which are typically a drab brown or grey colour, Flower Crab Spiders can be bright white and sunny yellow – perfect camouflage for many flowers. In fact, they can change colour to suit, although they're most often white.

Flower Crab Spiders don't spin a web like other spiders – instead they hide in plain sight, front legs outstretched, waiting for unlucky flies, bees or butterflies to land on their flower. Their strong front legs are ideal for ambushing bees busy collecting pollen. Although they're not the most common of spiders, you're likely to spot them as they primarily feed in the day when insects are buzzing around the flowers.

WILDFLOWER FOLKLORE

COW PARSLEY

Cow Parsley is one of those plants with lots of names, of which perhaps the prettiest is 'Queen Anne's Lace'. In the USA, this name refers to Wild Carrot (*Daucus carota*), which is sturdier and far less delicate than Cow Parsley (*Anthricus sylvestris*), a UK native that creates a froth of flowers throughout wild spaces in May and early June. It harks back to a folk tale that said that Cow Parsley flowers bloomed for Queen Anne and her ladies-in-waiting, and reflected the delicate lace they wore. It's also said they bloomed especially for Queen Anne in May, when she had a habit of travelling, and the verges and hedgerows lining the roads along which she passed were filled with these dainty flowers.

Most of the other common names for this delicate flower are more frightening: 'Mother Die', 'Mother's Death', 'Break-Your-Mother's-Heart', 'Devil's Bread' and 'Dead Man's Flourish'. These were used to scare children into thinking that their mother would die if they ever picked Cow Parsley. The idea was to stop children from touching deadly hemlock, which looks very similar, and it seems to have worked, as many people would not have Cow Parsley or anything resembling it in the house. The fact that Cow Parsley grows so freely in churchyards and on graves was another reason for fearing it. Lately, though, these pretty wildflowers have enjoyed a well-deserved resurgence in popularity among both florists and gardeners.

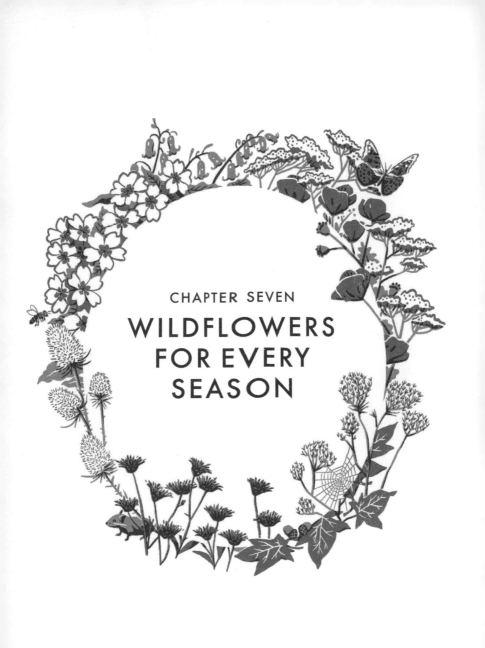

CHAPTER SEVEN

WILDFLOWERS FOR EVERY SEASON

The best thing you can do for wildlife by far is to make
sure you have plants in flower and fruit all year round.
That's hard to achieve unless you have acres of garden,
but you can go a good way towards it by growing as big a mix
of flowering plants, shrubs and trees as you can. Only planting
native wildflowers might not give you a huge list of options,
but it should cover most of the year – though you may want to
supplement with a few carefully chosen non-natives. Likewise,
sticking only to wildflowers might also limit your choice, even
if you include all the annuals, bulbs and herbaceous perennials,
so it's worth considering adding one or two shrubs and trees
if you can accommodate them. This is my guide to the best
wildflowers for each season that will suit most gardens and
grow happily without any fuss and bother. Bear in mind that
the list of additional plants at the end is not definitive, more
a handful of good suggestions.

SPRING

Spring flowers are often tough and hardy, withstanding cold
and rainy weather but also coping remarkably well with sudden
dry spells. Many of these flowers are great for planting in
containers and pots and a number, such as primrose and viola,
have been developed and bred into many colours and forms.
Be wary of these, though: they look similar to the wild species,
but are nowhere near as good for wildlife as they're often F1
hybrids – bred for flamboyant colour and size, and offering
little nectar or pollen. As a rule, stick to the species types of
flowers, which are certain to appeal to the broadest range
of wildlife.

UK AND EUROPE

Cowslip *Primula veris*

Banks and fields of bright yellow cowslips are a common sight in late spring, especially on chalk or limestone soils. Cowslips are important for wildlife, as their flowers provide an early source of nectar for various insects, including bees, beetles and butterflies, such as the Brimstone. Cowslip is also a food plant for the Duke of Burgundy butterfly.

Bluebell *Hyacinthoides non-scripta*

The English Bluebell is a dainty woodland carpeting bulb that is difficult, but not impossible, to naturalise in the garden, especially if you have a leaf mould-rich soil and plenty of dappled shade from overhead trees. What you are more likely to see in your garden, self-seeding all too freely, is the rampant Spanish Bluebell, a much more vigorous ruffian that is difficult to eradicate. Worryingly, it hybridises with the English Bluebell and may end up threatening its existence by outcompeting it and diluting the gene pool.

Red Campion *Silene dioica*

These easy-to-grow wildflowers add a super late-spring splash of rich pink-red to the garden. They love dappled shade such as under trees and hedges, or by a fence or wall, where their tall stems and vibrant flowers catch the eye, as well as the interest of various bees, butterflies and hoverflies.

Cow Parsley *Anthriscus sylvestris*

Frothy white flowers and ferny foliage make this late-spring flower a stunner. Cow Parsley is incredibly easy to grow from seed, even in poor soil, and is also happy in light shade or full sun, all of which make it a winner. The only downside is that the show is over by the middle of June.

MORE SPRING FLOWERS

Forget-Me-Not	*Myosotis* species
Snake's Head Fritillary	*Fritillaria meleagris*
Pasqueflower	*Pulsatilla vulgaris*
Wild Daffodil	*Narcissus pseudonarcissus*
Daisy	*Bellis perennis*
Dandelion	*Taraxacum officinale*
Lesser Celandine	*Ficaria verna*
Wood Anemone	*Anemone nemorosa*
Wild Garlic/Ramsons	*Allium ursinum*
Violet	*Viola* species
Dead Nettle	*Lamium* species
Buttercup	*Ranunculus* species

USA

Virginia Bluebells *Mertensia virginica*

A native wildflower found in moist woodlands and river flood plains. This ephemeral perennial plant comes up early in spring with purple-pink buds opening into sky-blue flowers with a delicate, sweet fragrance. The tubular flowers are favourites for pollinating bumblebees, as well as several types of butterfly, moth and hummingbird.

Dutchman's Breeches *Dicentra cucullaria*

Supposedly these look like pantaloons hanging upside-down to dry, but their inverted blossoms protect the pollen from wind and rain. Only female bumblebees with their long tongues can reach the nectar deep inside the spurs and pollinate the flower. They're easy to grow in the UK and Europe too.

Trout Lily *Erythronium americanum*

This easy-to-grow, early-blooming lily is a beauty with its yellow recurved petals. The purple splotches on its leaves resemble the markings on a Brook Trout, giving it its name. This also makes an elegant addition to UK and European gardens.

Red Trillium *Trillium erectum*

This striking plant has three heart-shaped leaves, three large red petals, and three green sepals. A woodland plant native to the USA, it goes by many common names, including 'Stinking Benjamin' – due to its rotting-flesh smell, which is meant to attract the flies that pollinate it – and 'Wake Robin', since it usually blooms around the time that robins return.

Cutleaf Toothwort *Cardamine concatenata*

A spring wildflower of moist forests and woods, this has spicy-tasting edible leaves and rhizomes, hence one of its other common names, 'Pepper Root'. The flowers are attractive to early-flying butterflies, and it makes a great addition to woodland gardens or borders.

MORE SPRING FLOWERS

Foamflower	*Tiarella cordifolia*
Bloodroot	*Sanguinaria canadensis*
Fire Pink	*Silene virginica*
Jack-in-the-Pulpit	*Arisaema triphyllum*
Solomon's Seal	*Polygonatum biflorum*
Liverleaf	*Hepatica nobilis*
Fringed Bleeding Heart	*Dicentra eximia*

SUMMER

Summer offers an array of brilliant wild blooms, from cheery Oxeye Daisies, poppies and buttercups, to elegant corncockles and rich blue cranesbills. Some of these, such as poppies, can be incredibly fleeting, grabbing their moment in the sun and attracting their preferred pollinator before setting seed and producing offspring. Others, such as Field Scabious, are long-lasting, providing consistent flushes of flowers into late summer. Many of the hay-meadow classic varieties, such as flowering grasses, cornflower and poppies, bloom early in summer, while others, including USA prairie favourites such as Black-Eyed Susan and echinacea, come into their moment in late summer.

UK AND EUROPE

Meadow Cranesbill *Geranium pratense*

The wild form of Meadow Cranesbill is a true summer beauty with its sky-blue flowers and mounds of beautifully cut, rich green leaves. So much so that there are many different named varieties to choose from, as well as the species. All are great for the garden and for wildlife, especially bees and moths.

Yarrow *Achillea millefolium*

Wild Yarrow produces white or soft-pink flat heads of flowers above feathery leaves all summer long and is very easy to grow. There are also lots of cultivated forms in all sorts of other colours, from yellow through to rich pink.

St John's Wort *Hypericum perforatum*

With its starry yellow flowers and sturdy stems, this wildflower's blooms last from June to September and is a magnet for pollinating insects.

Musk Mallow *Malva moschata*

This is such a beauty with its shell-pink, open flowers, and it's easy to grow in most gardens, especially on chalk or limestone soils.

Oxeye Daisy *Leucanthemum vulgare*

Simple and a super bloomer, the Oxeye Daisy can be somewhat invasive, colonising patches of the garden and self-seeding freely. It's happy in most soils and loves sunshine, but keep it within bounds.

MORE SUMMER FLOWERS

Mullein	*Verbascum* species
Corn Marigold	*Glebionis segetum*
Hawkbit	*Leontodon* species
Greater Stitchwort	*Rebelera holostea*
Hedge Garlic	*Alliaria petiolata*
Ribwort Plantain	*Plantago lanceolata*
Purple Loosestrife	*Lythrum salicaria*
Knapweed	*Centaurea* species
Common Vetch	*Vicia sativa*
Kidney Vetch	*Anthyllis vulneraria*
Meadow Vetchling	*Lathyrus pratensis*
Clover	*Trifolium* species
Cornflower	*Centaurea cyanus*
Yellow Rattle	*Rhinanthus minor*
Devil's-Bit Scabious	*Succisa pratensis*
Selfheal	*Prunella vulgaris*
Common Catsear	*Hypochaeris radicata*
Bird's-Foot Trefoil	*Lotus corniculatus*
Nipplewort	*Lapsana communis*
Fox and Cubs	*Pilosella aurantiaca*
Lady's Bedstraw	*Galium verum*
Meadowsweet	*Filipendula ulmaria*
Rosebay Willowherb	*Chamaenerion angustifolium*

USA

Black-Eyed Susan *Rudbeckia hirta*
A classic perennial for the garden with golden-yellow
daisy-like flower petals around a black central cone that
last from late summer into autumn, adding structure to
the late-season garden.

Purple Coneflower *Echinacea purpurea*
These resilient perennials have long-lasting, lavender-petalled
flowers surrounding a prickly orange cone that bloom from
midsummer until frost.

Sneezeweed *Helenium autumnale*
These easy-to-grow perennials flower right through to autumn
with sunny yellow flowers in their native form and rich reds
and rusty shades in their cultivated varieties. All are good for
bees and pollinators.

Wild Lupine *Lupinus perennis*
Found carpeting hillsides and meadows in the wild, this has
rich purple-blue flowers that make it great for the garden too.

California Poppy *Eschscholzia californica*
A favourite for dry gardens, the California poppy puts out
orange blooms that are popular with pollinators ranging
from bees to butterflies.

MORE SUMMER FLOWERS

New England Aster	*Symphyotrichum novae-angliae*
Wild Bergamot	*Monarda fistulosa*
Fireweed	*Chamaenerion angustifolium*
Goldenrod	*Solidago* species
Cardinal Flower	*Lobelia cardinalis*
Blazing Star	*Liatris* species
Blue Vervain	*Verbena hastata*
Jacob's Ladder	*Polemonium reptans*

AUTUMN AND WINTER

As the nights draw in, there is a final flurry of late flowers before most plants switch their focus to producing seeds and seed pods. But autumn does still bring the last blooms of scabious and knapweed, as well as the seed heads of teasels and thistles. In winter, while flowers may be few and far between, seeds and fruits come to the fore, providing hungry birds and mammals with a welcome meal.

UK AND EUROPE

Primrose *Primula vulgaris*

This harbinger of spring often flowers as early as December in the woods, hedgerows and grasslands where it grows wild. Primroses will keep on blooming until May and the soft, creamy flowers make a great addition to pots, borders and the bases of hedges. The flowers also attract pollinators such as Brimstone and Small Tortoiseshell butterflies.

Spear Thistle *Cirsium vulgare*

Although it flowers primarily from high summer through to autumn, don't be surprised to find this stocky, sturdy plant in flower during winter. It's a brilliant plant for wildlife – its purple thistle flowers are great for butterflies, and seed-eating birds, such as goldfinches, are drawn to them once they've set seed.

Lesser Celandine *Ficaria verna*

Appearing as early as January, this diminutive little wildflower keeps on blooming until May, producing masses of rich, shiny yellow flowers that are a valuable source of nectar for early insects. It's a good plant for awkward spots in the garden, such as under a hedge, where it colonises happily.

Teasel *Dipsacus fullonum*

The striking stems and seed heads of teasels last long after the plant has finished for winter. Those stems provide excellent shelter for insects and small mammals while the seed heads are a favourite with birds.

Snowdrops *Galanthus nivalis*

True winter flowers, snowdrops are easy to naturalise in moist, shady spots in the garden and its February flowers appear at just the right time for early insects.

MORE AUTUMN AND WINTER FLOWERS

Daisy	*Bellis perennis*
Autumn Hawkbit	*Leontodon autumnalis*
Common Toadflax	*Linaria vulgaris*
Field Scabious	*Knautia arvensis*
Devil's-Bit Scabious	*Succisa pratensis*
Stinking Hellebore	*Helleborus foetidus*
Winter Aconite	*Eranthus hyemalis*
Old Man's Beard	*Clematis vitalba*
Wild Daffodil	*Narcissus pseudonarcissus*

USA

Showy Milkweed *Asclepias speciose*

Showy Milkweed's dramatic seed pods ripen and burst open in early fall, adding drama to the garden. The preceding flowers are an important food source for many bees and butterflies.

White Prairie Aster *Symphyotrichum falcatum*

Fall is a time for asters on the prairies of the Great Plains and this wildflower also makes a great addition to the garden.

Swamp Sunflower *Helianthus angustifolius*

This plant's late-season golden flowers are a favourite with bees and are accented beautifully by dark green leaves.

Culver's Root *Veronicastrum virginicum*

After blooming all summer, with its white torches attracting tons of insects, Culver's Root leaves you with architectural stems that last all winter. It grows best in medium-to-moist soil with full sun.

Anise Hyssop *Agastache foeniculum*

Native to most of the northern USA, this drought-tolerant native has violet blooms that go on for months in summer. Insects love it. Its leaves smell like liquorice, while the winter stems and seed heads look great and provide food for birds and mammals.

MORE AUTUMN AND WINTER FLOWERS

Joe Pye Weed	*Eutrochium maculatum*
Blue False Indigo	*Baptisia australis*
American Senna	*Senna hebecarpa*
Wild Bergamot	*Monarda fistulosa*
Butterfly Weed	*Asclepias tuberosa*
Rattlesnake Master	*Eryngium yuccifolium*
American Dittany	*Cunila origanoides*
Long-Plumed Avens	*Geum triflorum*

SQUIRRELS AND TREES

Squirrels can be something of a nuisance in the garden, eating flower buds in spring and munching their way through food put out for birds. While their acrobatics can be very entertaining, most gardeners regard them as undesirable. But squirrels do perform an essential job in the natural world by burying their nuts in autumn and then forgetting where they are. This absent-mindedness plays an essential part in the spreading of oaks, pines and hickories, in particular.

Tree squirrels have shared a close history with many of the trees on which they depend for food, with both evolving together for their mutual benefit. At first glance, the relationship might appear somewhat one-sided, with squirrels benefitting from the trees for shelter and food in the form of acorns, nuts and other seeds. But the burying of their seeds offers trees a far greater range of dispersal than they could otherwise hope to achieve, especially during a 'mast year'. That's when oak trees, for example, produce an inordinate number of acorns, swamping the squirrel population with an abundance of food.

The squirrels madly bury them everywhere, spreading their caches far and wide and, ultimately, never going back because there are far too many for them to ever get around to eating, let alone remember where they are. As a result the trees hugely widen their range, ensuring their offspring are not growing in their parent's shadow and spreading their genes to achieve greater biodiversity. Clever.

WILDFLOWER FOLKLORE

ST JOHN'S WORT

You could easily pass this humble little wildflower without noticing, but it has a rich and varied history of magical powers, as well as real uses in herbal medicines that endure today. Native to the UK and Europe, and naturalised in the USA, St John's Wort has a variety of common names, including 'Devil's Scourge', 'Goatweed' and 'Touch-and-Heal', that bely its rather homely looks, suggesting its powerful place in the folk traditions of times gone by.

The name St John's Wort derives from the simple fact that it flowers around St John's Day, June 24, which made it readily available for all sorts of midsummer festivals and rituals, mainly focused on warding off evil spirits in the home. Everyone from the Ancient Greeks to St John the Baptist and later Christians used it to protect their houses, while farmers burned it to protect livestock from devils, goblins and witches, and it was also used as a medicinal remedy to cure 'demoniacs'.

Those practices have since fallen out of common usage, and St John's Wort was regarded as nothing more than a weed for a century or two, but you'll now find it in every herbal shop and pharmacy. It is a hugely popular herbal remedy, valued highly for its calming qualities and sometimes referred to as natural Prozac, after the popular tranquillizer.

CHAPTER EIGHT

RESOURCES AND READING LIST

It won't take you long to find a great deal of information, opinion and advice about wildflowers wherever you live – in the UK, Europe, the USA or elsewhere. Whatever your interest – growing wildflowers, buying seed, identifying flowers in the wild, discovering folklore and stories – you'll find plenty of websites, blogs and books to indulge your interest. In fact, it's so easy to slip down research rabbit holes reading up on wildflowers that it's a wonder this book isn't three times as long. I've listed my favourite resources here, but you are sure to find plenty more, with new sources popping up all the time. This list should help get you started finding your own rabbit holes to go down.

UK AND EUROPE

BOOKS

***Wild Flowers: of Britain and Ireland* by Roger Phillips**
A brilliant photographic guide to the wildflowers of the UK.

***Concise Wild Flower Guide* by Bloomsbury**
A very handy reference guide, excellent for taking with you on a walk.

***Flora Britannica* by Richard Mabey**
British folklore and wildflowers combine in this great book.

***Wild Flowers by Colour* by Marjorie Blamey**
A guide to identifying flowers in the UK and northwest Europe by their colour.

***How to Make a Wildlife Garden* by Chris Baines**
A brilliant how-to guide for all aspects of wildlife gardening.

WEBSITES

Woodland Trust Excellent tips on identifying wildflowers and what creatures enjoy them. woodlandtrust.org.uk

Plantlife All sorts of information on wildflowers and wild habitats in general. plantlife.org.uk

The Wildlife Trusts Information on habitats, events and much else. wildlifetrusts.org

Wild Flower Shop For wildflower seed and plugs. wildflowershop.co.uk

Emorsgate Seeds For wildflower lawn mixes. wildseed.co.uk

USA

BOOKS

National Geographic Pocket Guide to Wildflowers of North America **by Catherine H. Howell** A handy guide to 160 of the most common wildflowers from coast to coast, including Canada and Alaska.

The History and Folklore of North American Wildflowers **by Timothy Coffey** Wildflowers by family, including their common names, folklore and their uses for Native Americans.

WEBSITES

American Meadows Info, folklore, seed and much more. americanmeadows.com

Lady Bird Johnson Wildflower Center Masses of information on wildflowers across the USA. wildflower.org

Xerces Society Pollinator-Friendly Native Plant Lists Lists of pollinator-friendly plants and other useful information. xerces.org/pollinator-conservation/pollinator-friendly-plant-lists

Audubon Native Plants Database A database of native plants specific to zip code. audubon.org/native-plants

Pollinator Partnership Ecoregional Planting Guides A handy guide to plants for attracting bees and insects, tailored to your zip code. pollinator.org/guides

APPS

PlantNet Encyclopaedic app that covers the world, including Europe and the UK.

iNaturalist A kind of social network for nature lovers – upload a picture and get swift identifications of plants, animals and birds.

LeafSnap Contains high-resolution images of leaves, flowers, fruits, seeds and bark to aid identification.

A TO Z

COMMON NAMES

Many wildflowers have several common names, often local to a particular region or country. I've tried to include as many here as possible, but there will still be plenty more.

A

American Dittany	*Cunila origanoides*
American Senna	*Senna hebecarpa*
Angelica	*Angelica* species
Anise Hyssop	*Agastache foeniculum*
Arizona Lupine	*Lupinus arizonicus*
Autumn Hawkbit	*Leontodon autumnalis*

B

Baby Blue Eyes	*Nemophila menziesii*
Bachelor's Button	*Centaurea cyanus*
Betony	*Stachys officinalis*
Bird's-Eyes	*Gilia tricolor*
Bird's-Foot Trefoil	*Lotus corniculatus*
Black-Eyed Susan	*Rudbeckia hirta*
Bladder Campion	*Silene vulgaris*
Blazing Star	*Liatris spicata*
Bloodroot	*Sanguinaria canadensis*
Blue False Indigo	*Baptisia australis*
Blue Flax	*Linum perenne*
Blue Vervain	*Verbena hastata*
Borage	*Borago officinalis*
Break-Your-Mother's-Heart	*Anthriscus sylvestris*
Burdock	*Arctium* species
Buttercup	*Ranunculus* species
Butterfly Weed	*Asclepias tuberosa*

C

California Bluebell	*Phacelia minor*
California Poppy	*Eschscholzia californica*
Cardinal Flower	*Lobelia cardinalis*
Cheddar Pink	*Dianthus gratianopolitanus*
Cleavers	*Galium aparine*
Cock's-Foot	*Dactylis glomerata*
Colorado Blue Columbine	*Aquilegia coerulea*
Common Bent	*Agrostis capillaris*
Common Catsear	*Hypochaeris radicata*
Common Knapweed	*Centaurea nigra*
Common Toadflax	*Linaria vulgaris*
Common Vetch	*Vicia sativa*
Corncockle	*Agrostemma githago*
Cornflower	*Centaurea cyanus*
Corn Chamomile	*Anthemis arvensis*
Corn Marigold	*Glebionis segetum*
Cosmos	*Cosmos bipinnatus*
Cow Flop	*Digitalis purpurea*
Cow Parsley	*Anthriscus sylvestris*
Cowslip	*Primula veris*
Crested Dog's-Tail	*Cynosurus cristatus*
Cuckoo Flower	*Cardamine pratensis*
Culver's Root	*Veronicastrum virginicum*
Cutleaf Toothwort	*Cardamine concatenata*

D

Daisy	*Bellis perennis*
Dandelion	*Taraxacum officinale*
Dead Nettle	*Lamium* species
Dead Man's Bells	*Digitalis purpurea*
Dead Man's Flourish	*Anthriscus sylvestris*
Desert Marigold	*Baileya multiradiata*
Devil's Bread	*Anthriscus sylvestris*
Devil's-Bit Scabious	*Succisa pratensis*
Devil's Scourge	*Hypericum perforatum*
Dog Violet	*Viola canina*
Dutchman's Breeches	*Dicentra cucullaria*

E

English Bluebell	*Hyacinthoides non-scripta*
English Oak	*Quercus robur*
Evening Primrose	*Oenothera biennis*

F

Fairy Fingers	*Digitalis purpurea*
Field Forget-Me-Not	*Myosotis arvensis*
Field Scabious	*Knautia arvensis*
Fireweed	*Chamaenerion angustifolium*
Fire Pink	*Silene virginica*
Five Spot	*Nemophilia maculata*
Flapdock	*Digitalis purpurea*
Foamflower	*Tiarella cordifolia*
Forget-Me-Not	*Myosotis* species
Foxglove	*Digitalis purpurea*
Fox and Cubs	*Pilosella aurantiaca*
Fringed Bleeding Heart	*Dicentra eximia*

G

Garlic Mustard	*Alliaria petiolata*
Goatweeed	*Hypericum perforatum*
Globe Gilia	*Gilia capitata*
Goldenrod	*Solidago* species
Goose grass	*Galium aparine*
Greater Knapweed	*Centaurea scabiosa*
Greater Stitchwort	*Rebelera holostea*
Ground Elder	*Aegopodium podagraria*

H

Harebell	*Campanula rotundifolia*
Hawkbit	*Leontodon* species
Hedge Garlic	*Alliaria petiolata*
Hemp Agrimony	*Eupatorium cannabinum*

I

Indian Blanket   *Gaillardia pulchella*

J

Jack-by-the-Hedge   *Alliaria petiolata*
Jack-in-the-Pulpit   *Arisaema triphyllum*
Jacob's Ladder   *Polemonium reptans*
Joe Pye Weed   *Eupatorium maculatum*

K

Kidney Vetch   *Anthyllis vulneraria*

L

Lady's Bedstraw   *Galium verum*
Lady's Smock   *Cardamine pratensis*
Ladies' Thimbles   *Digitalis purpurea*
Lance-Leaf Coreopsis   *Coreopsis lanceolata*
Large-Leaved Lupine   *Lupinus polyphyllus*
Larkspur   *Consolida ajacis*
Lemon Beebalm   *Monarda citriodora*
Lesser Celandine   *Ficaria verna*
Lionsmouth   *Digitalis purpurea*
Liverleaf   *Hepatica nobilis*
Long-Plumed Avens   *Geum triflorum*
Lords and Ladies   *Arum maculatum*

M

Mayflower   *Cardamine pratensis*
Meadow Cranesbill   *Geranium pratense*
Meadowsweet   *Filipendula ulmaria*
Meadow Vetchling   *Lathyrus pratensis*
Mexican Hat   *Ratibida columnifera*
Milkmaid   *Cardamine pratensis*
Milkweed   *Asclepias* species
Mistletoe   *Viscum* species
Monkey Flower   *Erythranthe guttata*
Mother's Dead   *Anthriscus sylvestris*

Mother Die	*Anthriscus sylvestris*
Mouse-Ear Hawkweed	*Pilosella officinarum*
Mullein	*Verbascum thapsus*
Musk Mallow	*Malva moschata*

N

Nettle-Leaved Bellflower	*Campanula trachelium*
New England Aster	*Symphyotrichum novae-angliae*
Nipplewort	*Lapsana communis*

O

Old Man's Beard	*Clematis vitalba*
Opium Poppy	*Papaver somniferum*
Oxeye Daisy	*Leucanthemum vulgare*
Oxeye Sunflower	*Heliopsis helianthoides*

P

Pasqueflower	*Pulsatilla vulgaris*
Plains Coreopsis	*Coreopsis tinctoria*
Plantain	*Plantago* species
Primrose	*Primula vulgaris*
Poppy	*Papaver rhoeas*
Pot Marigold	*Calendula officinalis*
Purple Coneflower	*Echinacea purpurea*
Purple Loosestrife	*Lythrum salicaria*
Purple Toadflax	*Linaria purpurea*

Q

| Quaking Grass | *Briza media* |
| Queen Anne's Lace | *Anthriscus sylvestris* or *Daucus carota* |

R

Ramsons/Wild Garlic	*Allium ursinum*
Rattlesnake Master	*Eryngium yuccifolium*
Red Campion	*Silene dioica*
Red Clover	*Trifolium pratense*
Red Columbine	*Aquilegia canadensis*

Red Trillium   *Trillium erectum*
Ribwort Plantain   *Plantago lanceolata*
Rocky Mountain Bee Plant   *Cleome serrulata*
Rosebay Willowherb   *Chamaenerion angustifolium*
Russian Thistle   *Salsola tragus*

S

St John's Wort   *Hypericum perforatum*
Salad Burnet   *Sanguisorba minor*
Scotch Mercury   *Digitalis purpurea*
Selfheal   *Prunella vulgaris*
Showy Fleabane   *Erigeron speciosus*
Showy Milkweed   *Asclepias speciosa*
Snake's Head Fritillary   *Fritillaria meleagris*
Smooth Aster   *Symphyotrichum laeve*
Sneezeweed   *Helenium autumnale*
Snowdrop   *Galanthus nivalis*
Solomon's Seal   *Polygonatum biflorum*
Spanish Bluebell   *Hyacinthoides hispanica*
Spear Thistle   *Cirsium vulgare*
Spiked Speedwell   *Veronica spicata*
Squinancywort   *Asperula cynanchica*
Stinking Hellebore   *Helleborus foetidus*
Sunflower   *Helianthus annuus*
Swamp Milkweed   *Asclepias incarnata*
Swamp Sunflower   *Helianthus angustifolius*
Sweet Cicely   *Myrrhis odorata*
Sweet Woodruff   *Galium odoratum*

T

Tahoka Daisy   *Machaeranthera tanacetifolia*
Tall Tickseed   *Coreopsis tripteris*
Teasel   *Dipsacus fullonum*
Throatwort   *Digitalis purpurea*
Tickseed   *Coreopsis tinctoria*
Touch-and-Heal   *Hypericum perforatum*
Trout Lily   *Erythronium americanum*
Tumbleweed   *Salsola tragus*

U

V

Violets	*Viola* species
Viper's Bugloss	*Echium vulgare*
Virginia Bluebells	*Mertensia virginica*

W

Water Hyacinth	*Pontederia crassipes*
White Clover	*Trifolium repens*
Wild Bergamot	*Monarda fistulosa*
Wild Carrot	*Daucus carota*
Wild Daffodil	*Narcissus pseudonarcissus*
Wild Lupine	*Lupinus perennis*
Wild Marjoram	*Origanum vulgare*
Wild Strawberry	*Fragaria vesca*
Wild Thyme	*Thymus polytrichus*
Winter Aconite	*Eranthis hyemalis*
Witches' Gloves	*Digitalis purpurea*
White Prairie Aster	*Symphyotrichum falcatum*
Wood Anemone	*Anemone nemorosa*
Wood Avens	*Geum urbanum*

X

Y

Yarrow	*Achillea millefolium*
Yellow Rattle	*Rhinanthus minor*
Yew	*Taxus baccata*
Yorkshire Fog	*Holcus lanatus*

Z

Zigzag Goldenrod	*Solidago flexicaulis*
Zinnia	*Zinnia* species

ACKNOWLEDGEMENTS

My books would be just monochrome words without the wonderful illustrations of James Weston Lewis bringing everything to colourful life. Thank you, James.

Thanks, too, to Claire Harrup for populating each page so beautifully with a myriad of flowers and creatures in all her borders and detailed illustrations.

My thanks also go to the marvellous Harriet Butt, Maeve Bargman and the rest of the Quadrille team. As always, it's a joy working with you.

A 'thank you' is simply not enough for Jane Graham Maw and Maddy Belton at Graham Maw Christie for their constant support and unwavering enthusiasm, but it will have to suffice – thank you both.

Special thanks must go to Gerard Russell, wildflower farmer and my college friend, whose knowledge and enthusiasm was contagious then, and still is now.

Publishing Director Sarah Lavelle
Senior Commissioning Editor Harriet Butt
Series Designer Maeve Bargman
Cover and Chapter Opener Illustrations James Weston Lewis
Internal Illustrations Claire Harrup
Head of Production Stephen Lang
Production Controller Martina Georgieva

Published in 2024 by Quadrille, an imprint of Hardie Grant Publishing

Quadrille
52–54 Southwark Street
London SE1 1UN
quadrille.com

Cataloguing in Publication Data: a catalogue record for this book is available
from the British Library.

ISBN 978 183783 060 2

Printed in China using soy inks